W9-BLW-995

Mama's Going to Heaven Soon

by Kathe Martin Copeland

illustrated by Elissa Hudson

Dedicated to Robert and Sean,
whose mama went to heaven far too soon.
Love, Grammie

Dedicated to my mom,
who has always believed in me.
You made this possible.
Love, Lis

MAMA'S GOING TO HEAVEN SOON

Text copyright © 2005 Kathe Martin Copeland. Illustrations copyright © 2005 Elissa Hudson. All rights reserved. Except
for brief quotations in critical articles or reviews, no part of this book may be reproduced in any manner without prior
written permission from the publisher. Write to: Permissions, Augsburg Fortress, Box 1209, Minneapolis, MN 55440.

Large-quantity purchases or custom editions of this book are available at a discount from the publisher. For more information, contact the sales department at Augsburg Fortress, Publishers, 1-800-328-4648, or write to: Sales Director,
Augsburg Fortress, Publishers, P. O. Box 1209, Minneapolis, MN 55440-1209.

ISBN 0-8066-5122-9

The paper used in this publication meets the minimum requirements of American National Standard for Information
Sciences–Permanence of Paper for Printed Library Materials, ANSI Z329.48-1984. ⊚ ™

Manufactured in Singapore.

09   08   07   06   05   1   2   3   4   5   6   7   8   9   10

When a parent is terminally ill, it is important to explain the situation to young children in a clear and sensitive manner. When my son Todd and daughter-in-law Tammy faced Tammy's terminal breast cancer, they had trouble finding materials to help their young sons, ages five and three, understand the changes to come. I was inspired to create this book to offer a bit of comfort and understanding to my grand-sons and other young children. It is my fondest wish that this book would reach other families in their time of need.

A portion of the royalties from the sale of this book will be donated to the fight against cancer.

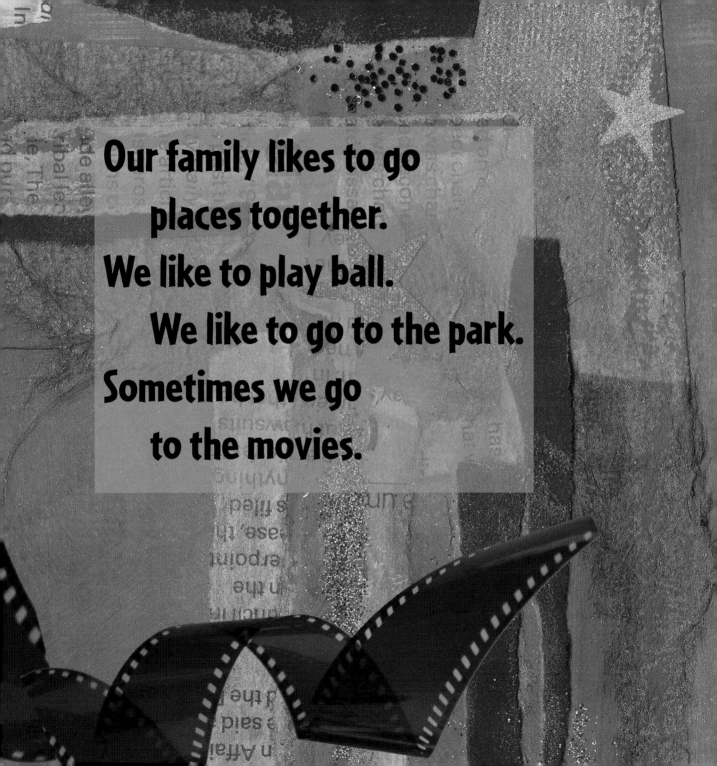

Our family likes to go
places together.
We like to play ball.
We like to go to the park.
Sometimes we go
to the movies.

Lately we've been staying home more because our mama doesn't feel very good. She's in bed a lot. We feel worried and sad. We want her to play with us. Sometimes she feels like playing. Other times she smiles and says she's just too tired.

People come to visit us,
but they look sad.
Sometimes they whisper or cry.
That makes us feel funny—
and we don't mean funny
like when you laugh.

We wish we could make our mama better.
We feel mad inside because
we don't know why our mama's sick
or why she doesn't get better.

Dance
Recital
MAY 10. Sat.
Row 10
Seat 4   FLOOR
"OnBroadway"

Last night our daddy told us
    that our mama is going to heaven soon.
"To live with God?" we asked.
    "Will she see some angels?"
"Yes," our daddy said.
    "Your mama is going to heaven,
and she will live with God and the angels."

"Oh boy!" we said.

"Can we go with her

and see God and the angels too?"

MAMA HEAVEN

"No," Daddy said.
"You are going to stay here on earth
as long as you are living.
We will still be a family
even though your mama is in heaven."

"How long will Mama be gone?" we asked.
"Forever," said Daddy.
"Your mama will not
come back here to live with us
after she goes to heaven."

"But why, Mama? Don't you love us anymore?"
"Don't you want to come back home and be with us?"

"My life on earth with you and Daddy will be over. I will live and stay in heaven forever, and I will never be sick or tired again."

Then Daddy said,
"Your mama will always be
a part of you and me
and everyone else that she loves.
We will always love your mama
and she will always love us—
even after she goes
to heaven.

"So you see,
even if you feel sad or scared
or worried or angry right now,
it's all right to feel that way.
Someday you will feel happy again.
You might still feel sad some of the time.
But when you do feel sad,
just remember how much your mama loves you."

"I will be here if you want to talk about being sad," said Daddy. "And so will all the other people who love you.

"Talking about how you are feeling will help you feel better inside.

Teacher

Minister

"You know, no matter how old you get, thinking about your mama— and about how much she loves you— will always make your heart smile."

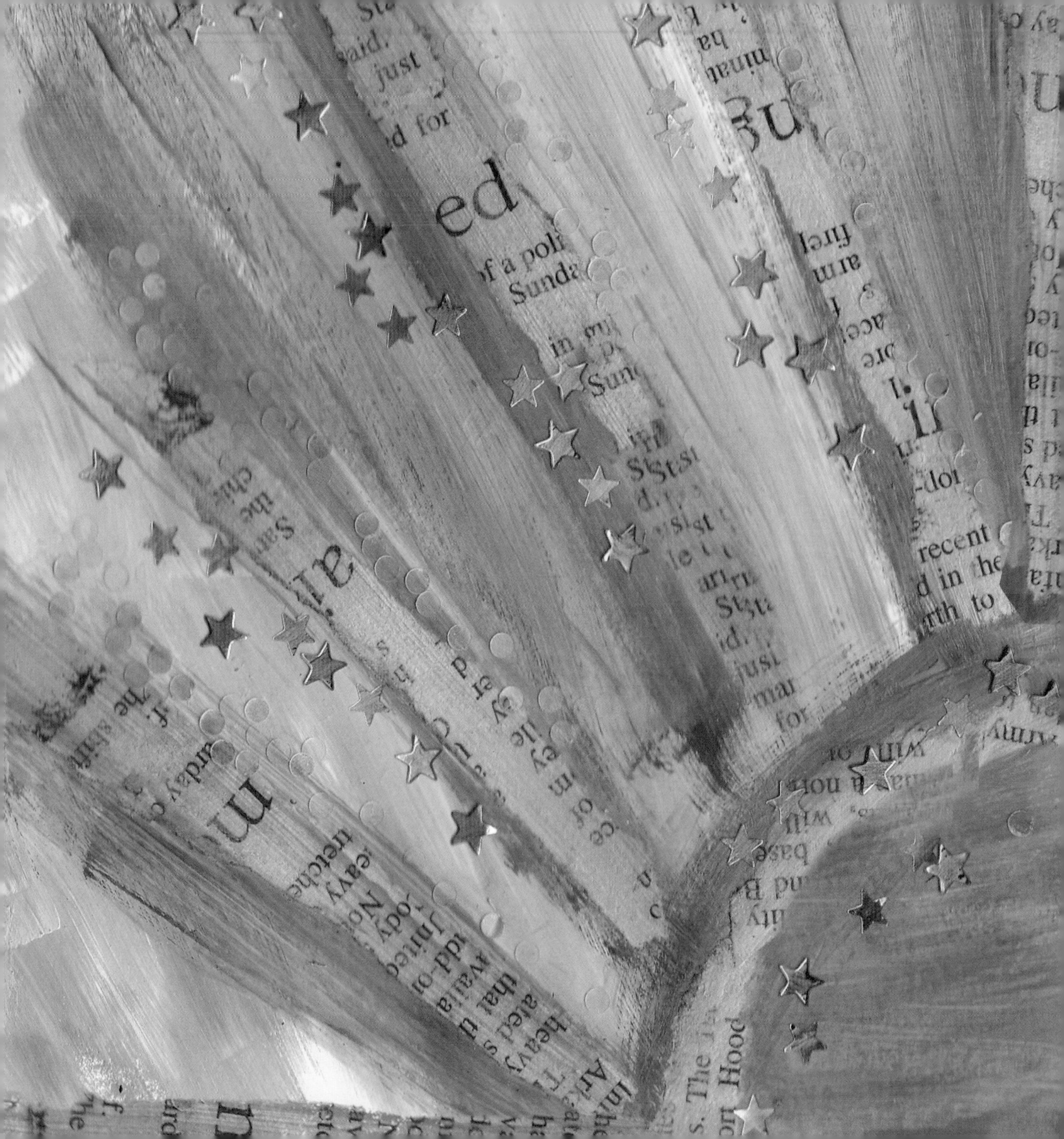

How to Talk to Children about Death

The following suggestions can help you discuss a loved one's death with your child. Be sure to adapt the information to meet your particular needs, being sensitive to the following factors:

- The age and maturity level of your child.
- Your child's past experiences with death—other relatives, pets, etc.
- Your child's relationship with the deceased.
- The circumstances of the death.
- Your child's typical way of coping with difficult situations.
- Your family's religious and cultural beliefs about death.

Use examples from nature to teach your child that death is a natural part of life. You might talk about seasons changing, plants growing and dying, or animal life cycles to show how death—while sometimes very sad—is part of life and how the world benefits from that life. It would be best to explore these ideas with your child before someone close to them dies, so he or she can learn about death from less-threatening situations.

Find a safe, quiet place to talk freely with your child. Avoid overloading your child with too many details. Provide only the basic information about the cause of death. Constantly assure your child that he or she will be safe. For example, if your loved one died from an illness, explain that it was a very serious illness, not like the illnesses that your child has had. If the death was caused by an accident, explain that the injuries were more serious than doctors could help and your loved one's body couldn't work any more.

Also assure your child that there are many people who love and will help them. Support from others will help them deal with the separation that accompanies death.

Invite your child to ask questions . . . but answer only what is being asked. Your child may wonder about what the body looks like or what will happen to the body, but be sure you understand the specific concern. Sometimes asking your child what he or she thinks the answer is will reveal what is bothering him or her—for example, whether your child wants a physical explanation of a burial or whether he or she is wondering about heaven.

Share your faith with your child. Explain that although we may see the loved one's body, the person's soul or spirit is no longer present. Share what your faith community believes happens to a person when he or she dies and what your personal beliefs are. Provide a comforting image for your child.

Children often "fill in the blanks" about what happens after death. They might imagine heaven to be a place in the sky filled with happy angels or people doing their favorite activities. It is often best not to contradict a child's description of heaven unless that image is disturbing or frightening. For example, you wouldn't want them to believe that God is a spiteful being who takes people to punish them or others.

Avoid describing God as a "taker." Saying "God took grandma to live in heaven" might make your child worry that God will take him or her away too. Instead, consider saying that while we don't know why people have to die, God is waiting with open arms to receive our loved ones.

Avoid saying, "It was God's will." This type of statement may confuse your child, especially if he or she thinks of God as kind and loving, watching over us like a parent. Parents do not want to hurt their children, so why would God? It is okay to say that we don't know why bad things happen. Assure children that God always loves us and is with us, even when we feel bad.

Use accurate language for death, not euphemisms. Children will be confused with the following terms: gone away, eternal rest, sleeping, passed on, lost, left us, or gone on a trip. Instead use direct expressions like dead, died, or stopped breathing to convey that the body is no longer physically alive.

Encourage children to express their feelings. Children look to trusted adults for direction and as models for behavior. If you openly share your feelings of sadness with your child, this will encourage him or her to do the same. Know that your child's grief may come in waves—crying one moment and then busily playing the next. Be ready to comfort and to assure your child.

However, if you are overwhelmed with your grief, take care not to frighten your child. Consider having someone familiar to your child come to your home to help you. This person can play or comfort your child while you are on a break. But avoid sending your child away from your home; he or she may feel excluded from sharing in the family's grief.

Try to follow your child's normal routine as much as possible. This will give your child a feeling of security. Avoid making drastic changes—such as moving to a new home or starting a new school—for up to one year. Such changes will add more stress to your child's life.

Seek help from friends, schools, churches, and hospitals. Some organizations may offer grief support groups for children; your child may benefit from talking with another child about his or her loss. Books and Internet sites also provide useful information on talking to your child. Counselors who specialize in grief can be very helpful, especially if your child has experienced intense feelings for an extended period of time.

—*Adapted with permission from Theresa M. Huntley's book* Helping Children Grieve: When Someone They Love Dies, *published by Augsburg Books (2002). Visit www.augsburgbooks.com for ordering information.*

This book is dedicated to Robert and Sean,
shown here planting kisses on their mother's head.